NEW YORK POST

Extra Hot
Su Doku

NEW YORK POST

Extra Hot
Su Doku

The Official Utterly Addictive

Number-Placing Puzzle

Compiled by Wayne Gould

Collins

An Imprint of HarperCollinsPublishers

HarperCollins books may be purchased for educational, busi-
ness, or sales promotional use. For information, please e-mail
the Special Markets Department at SPsales@harpercollins.com.

FIRST U.S. EDITION

ISBN: 978-0-06-137319-0
ISBN-10: 0-06-137319-2

16   RRD   20 19 18 17 16 15

Contents

Introduction

Since its launch in *The Times* in November 2004, Su Doku has become one of the most popular features of the paper and an international phenomenon. In a world where time is apparently a precious commodity, it is a testament to the addictive power of the puzzle that so many people can't wait to tackle it on a daily basis and with such intense concentration. *The Times* books, once they appeared in the bestseller lists, haven't budged since, showing their huge popularity with the book-buying public.

In this latest collection from Wayne Gould, you confront the ultimate mental workout. There are 150 new Extra Hot Su Dokus, ranging from very difficult to super fiendish, to test you to the absolute limit. Remember, these puzzles require no guesswork: logic will lead you to a single solution.

A valuable tip from Wayne Gould: 'If you are writing too many pencil marks, it means you are not understanding how the puzzle works. You may be relying too much on mechanical procedures, without appreciating the underlying logic. If, in time, you can shake yourself free of written pencil marks, you will see the Su Doku puzzle for what it is — a thing of beauty!'

Puzzles

				4	7	1		
5					3	7	6	
	4							
			9	5	6	2		
6								9
	2	5	1	6				
							5	
	9	1	5					8
		2	9	8				

Fiendish

2		5			4			
						8		3
	6			1		4	2	
					5	9		
4	7						1	6
		9	8					
	2	1		5			8	
5		3						
			4			1		7

Su Doku

	6						8	1
			3				9	6
	1			8	7		3	
			4					
3	5						6	9
					9			
	7		8	9			5	
1	3				6			
6	8						7	

Fiendish

			6					
3		9			7			
4	7			1				2
			2	6			8	
		1	8		9	3		
	6			7	5			
7				9			1	6
			1			7		8
					6			

Su Doku

	1						4	
		6		8		5		
7				1				2
	6		1		8		3	
9								7
	3		7		5		6	
3				5				1
		1		3		9		
	4						5	

Fiendish

	6					1		
		8	6				7	4
			7		5			
		4					6	
9		5	8		2	4		7
	2					5		
			1		9			
3	9				4	6		
		7					1	

					3	2		
		2		1	4		3	
1		5	7					6
	5							
		9	1		7	5		
							6	
4					2	9		1
	8		9	6		3		
		1	4					

Fiendish

		6		9	3			
			7		5	8		4
5								
3		2				7	8	
	6						2	
	1	8				3		9
								2
1		9	2		7			
			8	3		6		

Su Doku

4			3	9				1
		7		8			4	
	1				7			
		8	2					5
		6				8		
7					1	3		
			7				1	
	9			2		5		
8				1	3			2

Fiendish

						4	9	
		8				5		7
4				9	7			3
		9		2				1
			6		9			
3				5		7		
1			8	3				2
8		4				9		
	2	5						

Su Doku

	9			8		5		1
				2			3	
			9				4	2
4	1							
	6	5				3	1	
							8	4
2	4				7			
	7			9				
9		8		5			2	

Fiendish

		8			2		5	4
1							7	6
				1		9		
8		6			3			
			4		1			
			7			8		3
		4		7				
9	5							8
2	1		3			4		

1								3
	9		1				5	
2			4	3		1		
		5	7				1	
		9				3		
	8				9	6		
		1		7	5			6
	7				3		4	
5								9

Fiendish

		5		1		9		
			3		2			
1				8				3
	5		6		4		3	
9	6						1	7
	2		1		5		6	
8				3				4
			2		8			
		7		6		3		

Su Doku

	7			5			4	
3		2	1		4	8		9
8			5		6			4
				9				
1			8		7			3
2		3	7		9	6		8
	4			6			9	

Fiendish

	2			7	8			
	1			9		4		8
		7				3		
7		8	5					
				6				
					4	1		5
		5				7		
2		1		8			5	
			3	5			9	

Su Doku

			3	8	7			
	3			1			5	
4								3
9		2				5		4
		4	5		6	3		
3		6				8		1
6								2
	1			7			9	
			8	6	1			

Fiendish

	7				5		1	
4					8			9
		5		7		6		
7	9							
		2		6		5		
							8	4
		1		4		8		
2			8					3
	3		7				6	

Su Doku

		7	7	1				4
9			5		6			
							3	
8	3		6			1		
		5				9		
		1			4		7	8
	9							
			1		2			7
4				8		3		

Fiendish

					7			
1			5	2	4	3		
		8		9				5
8							5	
	3	7				9	6	
	4							2
6				7		5		
		9	2	1	8			4
			3					

Su Doku

		4				7	8	
				7				
9	1		3				6	
		6		3	5			7
	2						5	
8			9	2		3		
	6				1		9	2
				4				
	4	8				1		

	2		4					
3		7	1	6				5
					8	2		
		6						2
9		8				7		4
2						6		
		3	8					
6				7	4	9		3
					5		6	

Su Doku

	7		8		4	1	2	
	6	4		2				
3		1	5		9	8		9
7			1	2				4
	2			8			1	
5				8	3			1
7		4	3		8	4		0
				6		3	8	
	9	8	3		4		9	

Fiendish

	2		6		8		7	
7		8	9		1	6		3
4				2				7
	8						3	
1				8				5
6		1	8		5	4		2
	9		4		2		1	

Su Doku

1		5	7				3	
					5	4		2
						9		1
				2	9	8		
5								7
		6	5	3				
6		1						
2		7	8					
	8				4	7		6

Fiendish

	8		6			4		2
		4	9			3		
				2			5	
	4		5					
7								9
					6		1	
	2			7				
		7			3	2		
9		1			8		7	

9								
	4		3			2		5
				7			1	
					7	1		9
	5	9		8		7	3	
1		3	5					
	6			4				
8		1			5		9	
								2

Fiendish

			1					
3	1			6	5			
		4			2			5
2			5			6		
4		3				1		7
		7			1			3
7			2			5		
			7	4			9	6
					9			

						6	4	3
					7		5	
9				6				2
		2	1				3	
7			8		3			5
	3				5	9		
2				5				4
	6		9					
8	9	1						

Fiendish

5							2	3
	6		5	8		9		7
				4			1	
			8					9
		4				1		
7					4			
	8			1				
9		1		2	6		5	
3	5							1

		6		8		3		
8			5		9			1
9								2
		3	1		7	8		
		5	3		2	4		
5								3
6			7		3			8
		8		9		1		

Fiendish

2		8	9			4		
1				3				6
					2	9		
		6		2				
8	5						6	1
				5		8		
		9	1					
5				4				7
		3			9	5		8

2						6	9	
	6							
8			6			2	3	
		3	5	1			2	
			4		2			
	1			8	3	5		
	9	8			7			2
							4	
	2	7						5

Fiendish

	7						6	3
2			6					
	3		1		9			
3	6							9
			2		8			
1							7	8
		9			1		8	
					7			6
6	4						1	

	9		6					
		3	2	8				7
1						3		
					5			3
6	5		9		2		1	8
7			4					
		2						4
5				4	9	1		
					7		8	

Fiendish

				7		2	5	
						9	8	1
			3				7	
			6				2	7
		8	9		7	5		
5	7				3			
	4				1			
6	9	2						
	5	3		4				

	8		2			4		
					7			8
	9		3					1
6			5	3		1		
8								7
		9		6	2			3
4					3		7	
9			8					
		3			4		5	

Fiendish

	3				2	9		
6				4		7		
9			7					5
						1	9	
4			1		8			2
	2	9						
3					4			8
		5		7				3
		6	5				7	

Su Doku

			5					
	7			6	8			4
		5			2		7	
5					4	2		
		9				7		
		2	8					3
	9		1			6		
6			9	7			4	
				8				

Fiendish

		9		8	7			
			3			1		
	4							6
3				6			1	
6			7	9	4			5
	5			1				2
5							9	
		3			1			
			5	7		4		

6			9					
	8			7	4		3	
							7	1
7	5			1		4		
		8				7		
		3		4			6	5
9	6							
	7		5	3			2	
					2			6

Fiendish

4			9		7		2	
				1			7	6
				5		1		
	4					8		3
			3		4			
3		2					9	
		6		7				
2	1			4				
	7		6		9			5

Su Doku

		3		4		5		1
		6			2			
	4				3		2	
	9	8						
4		7				9		6
						2	4	
	5		9				1	
			7			8		
7		9		5		6		

Fiendish

	3			7	2			9
	8	1						
7			9				6	
			3	9		6		
			5		4			
		5		1	6			
	6				3			8
						1	4	
5			6	4			7	

		5	4					
8	2			9				
	4	3		5				9
9		7			4			
			5		8			
			9			1		7
1				3		9	7	
				6			1	3
					9	2		

Fiendish

			2					
7		5				3		
	4	8	3		6			
	9			6			8	1
				9				
5	1			2			9	
			4		9	1	2	
		7				9		4
					7			

Su Doku

				1			5	
					8	7		
		2		3		1	6	
9			1		7	6		
				5				
		7	8		4			1
	5	6		7		4		
		4	3					
	3			9				

Fiendish

					9		8	4
				4	1			
		7				6		
7			1			3		
8	3						1	7
		5			8			9
		2				4		
			3	2				
9	6		4					

			5			4		
								7
		9		7			5	
	1		4		8	3		2
4				1				5
5		6	2		3		7	
	7			3		9		
2								
		4			1			

Fiendish

8		3		5	7	2		
5			3				1	
				2				
3							4	
4	7						2	5
	2							6
				1				
	5				3			9
		9	6	7		5		2

	7			5				2
	8	2		4		3		
					6	8	7	
5				3				
		3				1		
				6				9
	4	7	6					
		5		2		7	8	
6				7			9	

Fiendish

			4			1		7
	4			9				
6					7			9
	5					8		2
			5		6			
8		3					5	
4			6					3
				3			4	
1		7		9				

Su Doku

			7					
7		1	9	8			6	
					1		8	4
	9		4			1		2
1		6			8		3	
6	1		2					
	7			6	9	2		5
					7			

Fiendish

							3	8
		9			5			
	3		7				9	
		2	9	4		3	6	
		1				8		
	5	3		7	2	9		
	8				7		4	
			4			1		
2	9							

Su Doku

	2		6					8
		4		3	8		9	
	3							
	7							3
5		2		9		4		1
6							8	
							5	
	5		7	8		1		
7					5		4	

Fiendish

	1					4		6
	4	8			7			3
			2				1	
4	6							9
			7		9			
3							6	8
	9				3			
1			5			6	3	
7		5					9	

Su Doku

6		9		1			2	
	5		4		2			
1					8			
		4	1				5	
	9						8	
	7				6	9		
			8					3
			3		4		9	
	3			5		1		8

Fiendish

			3		8	7		
	4	9		7				
		8			4			
7					5			9
9	5						3	2
8			6					1
			5			8		
				3		9	1	
		3	1		9			

Su Doku

6	7			4		1		
		1						
3				1			2	6
7				2	6			
	4						5	
			4	3				8
2	9			7				4
						8		
		5		8			7	2

Fiendish

			1		8		3	6
4	5		1		8		3	6
		7	4		6	2		
	8			6			5	
		6				8		
	7			9			6	
		2	6		7	1		
7	1		3		2		8	9

		4			6			
9	6		5	8		2		
					1	9		
	3	7						2
	8						4	
2						1	7	
		9	8					
		1		9	2		5	8
			3			6		

Fiendish

1			8	6				
	9			7			4	
		5				1	8	
5						4		
	3			6			9	
		2						8
	7	9				5		
	2			5			6	
			7	3				2

Su Doku

			9			7	
5			3					
	6	2						9
3	5			1				
6			4		2			5
				3			4	7
7						8	2	
					7			4
	9			5				

Fiendish

	3	1	2			6		
7		8			9			
			6				7	
6		4						
	1			7			4	
						5		3
	4				2			
			7			2		8
		7			5	3	1	

				9		5		
			6		8	7		9
							4	3
3			8			6		7
	6						1	
2		9			1			4
6	2							
9		4	3		5			
		8		2				

Fiendish

2				7			8	
	7					4		
		8			1	7		
7				6		3		
	9		4		3		1	
		5		2				9
		7	3			9		
		1					2	
	6			9				1

Su Doku

2	9		8					4
		1	4					
				5				9
1	4						3	
7			9		3			2
	3						5	8
3				7				
					2	4		
8					1		2	5

Fiendish

		2	1	5				
					6	7		
8					3		4	
4	7		8					
		5				3		
					7		8	4
	6		4					1
		1	2					
				9	1	5		

Su Doku

						2		
		5	7			6	9	4
			2	9				1
3		2					7	
			6		1			
	4					9		8
5				3	2			
6	2	1			4	8		
		8						

Fiendish

				6		9		
			5	1		4	2	
		4	2					
	6				5	8		
9		2				6		4
		1	7				9	
					8	2		
	1	7		5	2			
		6		7				

	8		6				2	
		7	5	3		8		
			7				1	
7								9
6			2		9			1
9								4
	7				6			
		4		2	5	7		
	6				8		9	

Fiendish

					1	4	2	
				6	5	8		
					9			6
7	5					2	6	
	3						4	
	2	8					5	3
8			4					
		3	6	5				
	7	9	8					

			3					
		3			2			5
	1	2		4				
3			6		9			8
		7				1		
6			1		7			4
				7		5	2	
8			4			7		
					6			

Fiendish

	7		5					6
3			1					5
				8			3	2
9					8			
		4				2		
			7					4
1	8			6				
4					9			8
5					3		2	

	1			2				
7					9	1		
5		6	8					
		1		8	5	9		
			1		4			
		5	9	6		3		
					3	2		6
		3	5					1
				7			4	

Fiendish

9					1	8		
				6			3	
2	1			4				9
				9	4			7
			1		6			
5			3	7				
6				1			2	8
	4			8				
		7	2					5

Su Doku

				2		3	1	6
		3				8		
1				5				
				1			7	4
	7		9		2		6	
5	1			6				
				9				3
		9				6		
3	2	1		4				

Fiendish

			2					
		8	1	6				
7	6					4	1	
4				5				
5	3						2	9
				1				6
	2	5					3	7
			3	8	9			
				6				

Su Doku

	5	8		4				
			7					5
6				1	5	9		
		7				8	3	
				3				
	4	6				7		
		5	2	6				7
2					8			
				5		4	6	

Fiendish

		7	6				3	
3				1		4		
1				3				8
5		4					6	
	9						1	
	7					3		4
8				4				3
		2		7				5
	6				9	8		

Su Doku

	6		8		2			
		5				9		7
	7						1	
6			1		7			2
				4				
5			3		9			8
	8						7	
3		4				6		
			5		1		3	

Fiendish

				4				9
4	2	1			6			
		3	5		8			
9	4			5				
			8		4			
				7			4	2
			4		7	5		
			2			1	3	8
5				8				

Su Doku

2			6		8			3
				5				
7		3				6		5
		4				2		
	2		7		9		4	
		6				1		
6		9				7		1
				7				
3			1		4			8

	6			2	8			1
2								4
			3		4		6	
		2			6			
		4		7		9		
			1			5		
	7		2		5			
3								9
1			8	6			2	

Su Doku

1					2	3	4	
	9			1	7			
2					8			
		6	2				3	
7								4
	3				9	1		
			8					6
			4	9			7	
	4	5	6					8

8								3
	7			3			9	
		5	4		9	1		
			9		5			
		2	8	7	4	3		
			2		3			
		4	1		2	8		
	8			5			2	
9								6

Su Doku

	4						2	
	8	6			9			1
					5			4
		8	5					2
		2	6		3	1		
9					7	5		
6			3					
1			9			3	8	
	3						5	

Fiendish

1		9			4	2		
	8				2		9	6
				1				
			3			5		
	4	1				3	7	
		8			7			
				2				
7	1		9				4	
		6	7			8		1

Su Doku

			7					
		6		8		9	4	
1					4			6
		9			8	4		2
		4				5		
7		5	9			6		
4			8					3
	5	8		1		2		
					3			

Fiendish

				8			1	7
		7	5					9
					6	2		
	8			3				5
	1	4				9	7	
5				9			2	
		2	3					
3					9	6		
1	9			6				

Su Doku

7	1							9
				2		3		
4			1					
					6		3	5
1			8		9			2
9	5		7					
					8			6
		8		6				
3							7	4

Fiendish

8				5		2		
4					8	3		
	6			2			1	
				9				4
	3	6				1	8	
1				8				
	7			3			5	
		2	5					8
		9		1				2

Su Doku

				6	3		4	8
				9		2		
						3		1
	7	9	3					
1		4				9		3
					8	1	7	
6		7						
		8		2				
3	1		5	8				

Fiendish

	4			5				
					9		2	
	5	6					1	4
4				9	6	3		
			7		2			
		9	4	3				6
5	3					1	8	
	8		1					
				2			6	

Su Doku

		1	6	2	8			9
								8
		4				6	2	
			4			1		
9				5				3
		6			3			
	8	2				9		
1								
6			7	3	5	2		

Fiendish

		7				3		
			1		4			
	6	3	5		9	1	2	
	5	8				7	9	
	9	4				2	3	
	4	5	6		8	9	1	
			4		1			
		9				4		

Su Doku

6				3				9
		4			1			
		7					3	
		6	3	7				2
	9		6		8		1	
7				1	9	8		
	5					2		
			1			7		
8				9				4

Fiendish

	1	6				8		
		9	5			6		
5							4	
			2	3			5	
		8		7		4		
	7			6	4			
	6							4
		7			1	9		
		1				7	2	

Su Doku

			3			6		
		7	8		4		3	
				9			5	
		6	1					
	7	2		6		4	1	
					9	7		
	8			5				
	4		2		8	9		
		3			6			

Fiendish

8	4						1	9
		3	7		1	4		
	5		4	2	8		9	
				6				
	2		3	1	9		8	
		9	8		2	3		
6	7						4	5

Su Doku

1				7	6		9	
		6	2			8		
				5				4
2	9	4						
	3						4	
						3	5	2
7				4				
		2			1	6		
	8		3	2				1

Fiendish

	6			7	1			2
					2		6	
	5					4		
1		8	2					9
				8				
4					6	5		8
		4					2	
	7		3					
9			7	2			8	

Su Doku

	9							
1				7	6		4	2
7		3	4					
	8	9					1	
			1		2			
	3					2	6	
					5	4		8
3	4		2	6				1
							7	

Fiendish

5				4		9		
6		7	2			5		
9							4	
		3	9					
	1			2			5	
					8	7		
	2							6
		8			3	1		2
		4		8				5

Su Doku

		9		8	1		2	
				9				7	5
1		5			8		4	
	2						9	4
			2		6			
4	1						2	
	5		7			8		6
	3			5				
			9			2		

Fiendish

	2			8				
5	9							
				2	5	7		8
	3		1			6		4
		1				5		
4		2			8		7	
2		3	4	1				
							1	9
				7			6	

	2						1	
1			2		7			3
		5				2		
	3			6			9	
8			9		4			2
	1			7			4	
		3				5		
2			8		5			4
	6						3	

					3			5
7	6			1				
			4			9		1
	5			3	2			
3	8						1	7
			7	8			9	
4		9			5			
				7			3	9
6			2					

Su Doku

		4		5	8		7	
9								
1				6		4		
3	5				6			1
				4				
7			8				5	3
		3		2				5
								2
	2		7	9		6		

Fiendish

			3					9
9	4	5		6				
			5				2	
6						8	1	
		2		3		9		
	8	4						6
	6				1			
				5		7	4	1
1					8			

Su Doku

6	8						3	
			2					6
3				6				
8		6	1			9		
	9			2			7	
		7			6	3		2
				5				7
4					1			
	3						8	4

Fiendish

		6		3				
7								
4	8					6		9
		4		9	8	2		
			6		5			
		3	4	1		8		
5		9					6	7
								1
				2		4		

Su Doku

	2			7			8	
	6	8						5
		5		9				4
		1			6			
5			2		1			9
			9			4		
1				2		3		
2						8	5	
	7			6			9	

Fiendish

		1	5				3	
			7		2			8
	2					6		5
					7		8	
8	7						4	2
	5		9					
6		2					9	
9			3		1			
	4				6	1		

Su Doku

8			4	5		9		
			3			5		6
								2
9			1				5	
		6	9		4	8		
	3				2			9
3								
4		1			5			
		7		1	9			4

Fiendish

			6	9			7	5
			7		8			
4						2		
3			8					6
		4		7		3		
8					9			4
		3						9
			9		5			
6	1			8	2			

Su Doku

9					5			
4		1		8				
		3						2
		5	4			7		
		6		7		8		
		2			9	4		
6						1		
				4		6		3
			5					4

Fiendish

			3				8	2
8				5		4		9
	9			2				
6		4			3			
				7				
		5				2		1
				9			5	
4		9		1				8
2	7				5			

Su Doku

		5		2				9
				8			3	
1	7		9					
4	3							8
		2				3		
9							1	4
					8		9	2
	1			3				
6				5		1		

Fiendish

3		5	9	2				7
4	6							
	2				8		3	
	1	4						
8								5
						9	2	
	7		1				4	
							5	9
5				7	6	3		2

Su Doku

	7			9				
			2			8		
1	5		8		6			
	1							8
	8		7		2		9	
6							5	
			4		9		8	6
		3			5			
				3			4	

Fiendish

			3	7	9			
6								4
	7						5	
8		4		9		2		5
9		5		2		3		7
	1						3	
5								2
			1	4	6			

Su Doku

		4	5			8		
	3				9			
			2					1
		1		6			3	
3		2				4		9
	9			1		6		
4					6			
			8				7	
		8			7	9		

Fiendish

3							4	
			8	1				3
5		4	3			2		
6			9	3				
	7						2	
				7	8			9
		6			3	4		7
8				5	9			
	1							8

Su Doku

	9							
			2					8
5	8	6		7				
6			1		8	3		
9	4						1	7
	2		6		7			9
				5		1	6	4
7					4			
							2	

Fiendish

				8				
					3	4	2	5
	9			2		1		6
	7			9	1			2
2			8	3			7	
7		2		1			9	
1	5	3	2					
				7				

Su Doku

				5	9			2
			4				3	
	2	9			3	6	5	
		6						
	1	8				5	7	
						4		
	4	5	2			1	6	
	6				4			
3			1	7				

Fiendish

			2		4			
5			3		9			4
		2		7		5		
8	7						9	5
		5				1		
4	6						8	3
		3		6		8		
1			9		5			7
			8		1			

Su Doku

		3			8	6		
2	7		4			8		
1				2				
7	1							3
		5				1		
8							2	9
				1				6
		1			9		5	4
		6	3			2		

Fiendish

	5					1		9
	8	6	5					
	4		3					
5			4					
	6	9		3		4	8	
					9			2
					6		3	
					2	8	9	
4		8					2	

Su Doku

	3				6		5	
			9		3	6		2
5			8				9	
						9		8
	4						2	
8		1						
	9				8			5
4		5	7		1			
	8		6				1	

Fiendish

	2			1	7			6
							2	8
5		4	1		3	7		
	7			2			6	
		2	6		9	5		1
3	5							
2			9	4			1	

Su Doku

	5		6		9			
6				3				
7		8	4					
	8	5		4				
	7						9	
				9		8	3	
					6	2		7
				8				1
			1		3		6	

Fiendish

		3	1				5	
				7	5	1		
		6			3	9		
9	3	4						
				8				
						3	4	2
		7	8			5		
		8	5	3				
	4				9	6		

Su Doku

		2	8		9	5		8
7	6						9	
				8		6	5	
				7		8		3
			1		3			
3		7		2				
	9	4		1				
	8						4	1
5			6			9		

Fiendish

		5		4	8			
	7							3
	4		5					
8				1		6		
2			4		5			1
		4		6				7
					3		8	
4							7	
			8	2		9		

Su Doku

5	3				9			1
7			5					
		8			2	3		
				4	5			
	5	3				8	9	
			8	9				
		6	2			9		
					6			4
9			7				3	2

Fiendish

		9		2		6		
	5				4	7		
8							3	9
			3					1
		7	2		9	3		
9					5			
4	3							2
		5	7				4	
		6		1		8		

Su Doku

				6		2		
	4		3					6
6		5		4				3
8		3	2					
	5						8	
					8	6		9
9				5		3		8
4					9		6	
		1		7				

Fiendish

			1		6		4	9
9		7		4	3			
3								
	7					6		2
4		1					8	
								5
			6	3		4		8
8	2		7		1			

Su Doku

5			8		4			2
	1	8				6	9	
6				2				3
	5	3				7	2	
8				9				4
	6	9				1	4	
3			1		7			9

Fiendish

8								7
	1	5		8				4
	9					5	6	
				9	8			
			3	4	5			
			7	1				
	6	4					9	
5				3		2	7	
3								6

Su Doku

	3	4					6	
				6		8		
2	6	1						7
				2	6	9		
	8						3	
		6	9	4				
5						1	9	2
		8		7				
	4					7	8	

Fiendish

4				6		3		9
				3				1
	3					7		
		1	5			2		
	7							6
		5			4	8		
		7					8	
8				4				
5		9		7				3

Su Doku

6								
				5		6	4	9
5	2				9	8		
	7	3			6			
			8			4	2	
		4	5				3	8
8	5	6		1				
								5

Fiendish

		2		9		5		
4	9		5					
		3			1			4
	4				3			
2			8		9			7
			4				5	
8			6			2		
				7			6	3
		6		4		8		

8	2		7	4				
1								
5			2				1	
	4			7	9			
		3				5		
			3	1			2	
	9				4			7
								8
			5	7			3	2

Fiendish

4				1			7	
5				9				
2		8			4			
	3	5				6		8
8		9				5	3	
			1			8		6
				7				3
	6			4				7

Su Doku

9				6	3			
	3		1				7	
7		6						
5				9	2			
		4				1		
			4	5				3
						2		7
	9				7		3	
			5	8				9

Fiendish

							9	
	2			9	6	8		
	1		7		3			
		6		3		7		
4	3						2	9
		1		5		6		
			9		1		5	
		7	4	2			6	
	9							

Su Doku

Solutions

Solutions

1

2	3	6	8	4	7	1	9	5
5	8	9	2	1	3	7	6	4
1	4	7	6	5	9	8	3	2
8	7	3	4	9	5	6	2	1
6	1	4	7	3	2	5	8	9
9	2	5	1	6	8	4	7	3
4	6	8	3	2	1	9	5	7
3	9	1	5	7	6	2	4	8
7	5	2	9	8	4	3	1	6

2

2	8	5	3	7	4	6	9	1
9	1	4	5	2	6	8	7	3
3	6	7	9	1	8	4	2	5
1	3	2	7	6	5	9	4	8
4	7	8	2	9	3	5	1	6
6	5	9	8	4	1	7	3	2
7	2	1	6	5	9	3	8	4
5	4	3	1	8	7	2	6	9
8	9	6	4	3	2	1	5	7

Solutions

7	6	3	9	5	4	2	8	1
5	4	8	3	1	2	7	9	6
9	1	2	6	8	7	5	3	4
8	9	1	4	6	5	3	2	7
3	5	7	1	2	8	4	6	9
4	2	6	7	3	9	8	1	5
2	7	4	8	9	1	6	5	3
1	3	5	2	7	6	9	4	8
6	8	9	5	4	3	1	7	2

5	1	2	6	8	4	9	7	3
3	8	9	5	2	7	6	4	1
4	7	6	9	1	3	8	5	2
9	3	7	2	6	1	4	8	5
2	5	1	8	4	9	3	6	7
8	6	4	3	7	5	1	2	9
7	2	3	4	9	8	5	1	6
6	4	5	1	3	2	7	9	8
1	9	8	7	5	6	2	3	4

Solutions

5

5	1	3	2	6	9	7	4	8
2	9	6	4	8	7	5	1	3
7	8	4	5	1	3	6	9	2
4	6	7	1	9	8	2	3	5
9	2	5	3	4	6	1	8	7
1	3	8	7	2	5	4	6	9
3	7	9	6	5	4	8	2	1
6	5	1	8	3	2	9	7	4
8	4	2	9	7	1	3	5	6

6

7	6	9	4	2	8	1	5	3
1	5	8	6	9	3	2	7	4
4	3	2	7	1	5	8	9	6
8	7	4	3	5	1	9	6	2
9	1	5	8	6	2	4	3	7
6	2	3	9	4	7	5	8	1
2	8	6	1	3	9	7	4	5
3	9	1	5	7	4	6	2	8
5	4	7	2	8	6	3	1	9

7

8	4	6	5	9	3	2	1	7
9	7	2	6	1	4	8	3	5
1	3	5	7	2	8	4	9	6
7	5	4	3	8	6	1	2	9
6	2	9	1	4	7	5	8	3
3	1	8	2	5	9	7	6	4
4	6	3	8	7	2	9	5	1
5	8	7	9	6	1	3	4	2
2	9	1	4	3	5	6	7	8

8

8	7	6	4	9	3	2	1	5
2	9	3	7	1	5	8	6	4
5	4	1	6	8	2	9	7	3
3	5	2	1	4	9	7	8	6
9	6	4	3	7	8	5	2	1
7	1	8	5	2	6	3	4	9
6	8	7	9	5	4	1	3	2
1	3	9	2	6	7	4	5	8
4	2	5	8	3	1	6	9	7

Solutions

9

4	8	2	3	9	6	7	5	1
5	6	7	1	8	2	9	4	3
3	1	9	5	4	7	2	8	6
9	3	8	2	7	4	1	6	5
1	2	6	9	3	5	8	7	4
7	5	4	8	6	1	3	2	9
2	4	3	7	5	9	6	1	8
6	9	1	4	2	8	5	3	7
8	7	5	6	1	3	4	9	2

10

2	7	3	5	8	1	4	9	6
9	1	8	3	4	6	5	2	7
4	5	6	2	9	7	1	8	3
7	6	9	4	2	3	8	5	1
5	8	1	6	7	9	2	3	4
3	4	2	1	5	8	7	6	9
1	9	7	8	3	5	6	4	2
8	3	4	7	6	2	9	1	5
6	2	5	9	1	4	3	7	8

Solutions

6	9	2	4	8	3	5	7	1
7	5	4	1	2	6	9	3	8
1	8	3	9	7	5	6	4	2
4	1	7	8	3	9	2	5	6
8	6	5	7	4	2	3	1	9
3	2	9	5	6	1	7	8	4
2	4	6	3	1	7	8	9	5
5	7	1	2	9	8	4	6	3
9	3	8	6	5	4	1	2	7

7	6	8	9	3	2	1	5	4
1	2	9	8	4	5	3	7	6
4	3	5	6	1	7	9	8	2
8	4	6	5	9	3	2	1	7
3	7	2	4	8	1	6	9	5
5	9	1	7	2	6	8	4	3
6	8	4	2	7	9	5	3	1
9	5	3	1	6	4	7	2	8
2	1	7	3	5	8	4	6	9

Solutions

13

1	4	7	5	9	2	8	6	3
8	9	3	1	6	7	4	5	2
2	5	6	4	3	8	1	9	7
3	2	5	7	8	6	9	1	4
6	1	9	2	5	4	3	7	8
7	8	4	3	1	9	6	2	5
4	3	1	9	7	5	2	8	6
9	7	8	6	2	3	5	4	1
5	6	2	8	4	1	7	3	9

14

4	3	5	7	1	6	9	2	8
6	8	9	3	5	2	7	4	1
1	7	2	4	8	9	6	5	3
7	5	1	6	9	4	8	3	2
9	6	4	8	2	3	5	1	7
3	2	8	1	7	5	4	6	9
8	1	6	5	3	7	2	9	4
5	9	3	2	4	8	1	7	6
2	4	7	9	6	1	3	8	5

Solutions

15

4	8	5	9	3	2	1	7	6
9	7	1	6	5	8	3	4	2
3	6	2	1	7	4	8	5	9
8	3	7	5	1	6	9	2	4
5	2	6	4	9	3	7	8	1
1	9	4	8	2	7	5	6	3
2	5	3	7	4	9	6	1	8
7	4	8	3	6	1	2	9	5
6	1	9	2	8	5	4	3	7

16

3	2	9	4	7	8	5	1	6
5	1	6	2	9	3	4	7	8
4	8	7	6	1	5	3	2	9
7	4	8	5	2	1	9	6	3
1	5	3	8	6	9	2	4	7
9	6	2	7	3	4	1	8	5
8	9	5	1	4	6	7	3	2
2	3	1	9	8	7	6	5	4
6	7	4	3	5	2	8	9	1

Solutions

17

5	2	1	3	8	7	9	4	6
7	3	9	6	1	4	2	5	8
4	6	8	2	9	5	7	1	3
9	7	2	1	3	8	5	6	4
1	8	4	5	2	6	3	7	9
3	5	6	7	4	9	8	2	1
6	4	7	9	5	3	1	8	2
8	1	3	4	7	2	6	9	5
2	9	5	8	6	1	4	3	7

18

6	7	8	4	9	5	3	1	2
4	1	3	6	2	8	7	5	9
9	2	5	1	7	3	6	4	8
7	9	4	5	8	1	2	3	6
3	8	2	9	6	4	5	7	1
1	5	6	2	3	7	9	8	4
5	6	1	3	4	9	8	2	7
2	4	7	8	5	6	1	9	3
8	3	9	7	1	2	4	6	5

Solutions

19

3	8	7	2	1	9	6	5	4
9	2	4	5	3	6	7	8	1
5	1	6	4	7	8	2	3	9
8	3	9	6	5	7	1	4	2
7	4	5	8	2	1	9	6	3
2	6	1	3	9	4	5	7	8
1	9	8	7	6	3	4	2	5
6	5	3	1	4	2	8	9	7
4	7	2	9	8	5	3	1	6

20

5	9	3	1	8	7	2	4	6
1	7	6	5	2	4	3	9	8
4	2	8	6	9	3	7	1	5
8	6	1	9	3	2	4	5	7
2	3	7	8	4	5	9	6	1
9	4	5	7	6	1	8	3	2
6	1	2	4	7	9	5	8	3
3	5	9	2	1	8	6	7	4
7	8	4	3	5	6	1	2	9

Solutions

21

5	3	4	2	1	6	7	8	9
6	8	2	4	7	9	5	1	3
9	1	7	3	5	8	2	6	4
4	9	6	1	3	5	8	2	7
7	2	3	8	6	4	9	5	1
8	5	1	9	2	7	3	4	6
3	6	5	7	8	1	4	9	2
1	7	9	5	4	2	6	3	8
2	4	8	6	9	3	1	7	5

22

8	2	1	4	5	9	3	7	6
3	4	7	1	6	2	8	9	5
5	6	9	7	3	8	2	4	1
7	5	6	9	4	3	1	8	2
9	3	8	6	2	1	7	5	4
2	1	4	5	8	7	6	3	9
4	9	3	8	1	6	5	2	7
6	8	5	2	7	4	9	1	3
1	7	2	3	9	5	4	6	8

23

3	5	7	6	9	4	1	2	8
9	6	4	8	2	1	7	5	3
2	8	1	5	3	7	6	4	9
8	7	6	1	5	2	9	3	4
4	2	3	9	8	6	5	1	7
5	1	9	4	7	3	8	6	2
7	3	5	2	1	8	4	9	6
1	4	2	7	6	9	3	8	5
6	9	8	3	4	5	2	7	1

24

9	2	4	6	3	8	5	7	1
3	1	6	2	5	7	8	4	9
7	5	8	9	4	1	6	2	3
4	6	3	5	2	9	1	8	7
2	8	5	7	1	6	9	3	4
1	7	9	3	8	4	2	6	5
6	3	1	8	7	5	4	9	2
8	4	2	1	9	3	7	5	6
5	9	7	4	6	2	3	1	8

Solutions

25

1	9	5	7	4	2	6	3	8
3	6	8	9	1	5	4	7	2
4	7	2	3	6	8	9	5	1
7	3	4	6	2	9	8	1	5
5	2	9	4	8	1	3	6	7
8	1	6	5	3	7	2	9	4
6	4	1	2	7	3	5	8	9
2	5	7	8	9	6	1	4	3
9	8	3	1	5	4	7	2	6

26

1	8	3	6	5	7	4	9	2
2	5	4	9	8	1	3	6	7
6	7	9	3	2	4	1	5	8
8	4	6	5	1	9	7	2	3
7	1	5	8	3	2	6	4	9
3	9	2	7	4	6	8	1	5
4	2	8	1	7	5	9	3	6
5	6	7	4	9	3	2	8	1
9	3	1	2	6	8	5	7	4

Solutions

27

9	1	7	8	5	2	6	4	3
6	4	8	3	9	1	2	7	5
3	2	5	4	7	6	9	1	8
4	8	6	2	3	7	1	5	9
2	5	9	1	8	4	7	3	6
1	7	3	5	6	9	8	2	4
7	6	2	9	4	3	5	8	1
8	3	1	6	2	5	4	9	7
5	9	4	7	1	8	3	6	2

28

5	2	9	1	7	4	3	6	8
3	1	8	9	6	5	4	7	2
6	7	4	3	8	2	9	1	5
2	8	1	5	3	7	6	4	9
4	5	3	8	9	6	1	2	7
9	6	7	4	2	1	8	5	3
7	9	6	2	1	3	5	8	4
1	3	5	7	4	8	2	9	6
8	4	2	6	5	9	7	3	1

Solutions

29

1	2	7	5	8	9	6	4	3
3	4	6	2	1	7	8	5	9
9	5	8	3	6	4	7	1	2
5	8	2	1	9	6	4	3	7
7	1	9	8	4	3	2	6	5
6	3	4	7	2	5	9	8	1
2	7	3	6	5	8	1	9	4
4	6	5	9	7	1	3	2	8
8	9	1	4	3	2	5	7	6

30

5	4	8	1	9	7	6	2	3
1	6	3	5	8	2	9	4	7
2	9	7	6	4	3	5	1	8
6	2	5	8	3	1	4	7	9
8	3	4	7	5	9	1	6	2
7	1	9	2	6	4	3	8	5
4	8	2	9	1	5	7	3	6
9	7	1	3	2	6	8	5	4
3	5	6	4	7	8	2	9	1

Solutions

4	7	6	2	8	1	3	9	5
8	3	2	5	7	9	6	4	1
9	5	1	4	3	6	7	8	2
2	9	3	1	4	7	8	5	6
1	6	4	9	5	8	2	3	7
7	8	5	3	6	2	4	1	9
5	1	7	8	2	4	9	6	3
6	4	9	7	1	3	5	2	8
3	2	8	6	9	5	1	7	4

2	3	8	9	6	7	4	1	5
1	9	5	4	3	8	7	2	6
4	6	7	5	1	2	9	8	3
9	7	6	8	2	1	3	5	4
8	5	4	7	9	3	2	6	1
3	2	1	6	5	4	8	7	9
7	4	9	1	8	5	6	3	2
5	8	2	3	4	6	1	9	7
6	1	3	2	7	9	5	4	8

Solutions

33

2	3	5	7	4	1	6	9	8
9	6	1	2	3	8	4	5	7
8	7	4	6	9	5	2	3	1
7	4	3	5	1	6	8	2	9
5	8	9	4	7	2	3	1	6
6	1	2	9	8	3	5	7	4
4	9	8	3	5	7	1	6	2
1	5	6	8	2	9	7	4	3
3	2	7	1	6	4	9	8	5

34

9	7	5	4	8	2	1	6	3
2	1	4	6	9	3	8	5	7
8	3	6	1	7	5	9	4	2
3	6	8	7	1	4	5	2	9
4	9	7	2	5	8	6	3	1
1	5	2	9	3	6	4	7	8
7	2	9	5	6	1	3	8	4
5	8	1	3	4	7	2	9	6
6	4	3	8	2	9	7	1	5

Solutions

35

2	9	5	6	7	3	8	4	1
4	6	3	2	8	1	5	9	7
1	8	7	5	9	4	3	2	6
9	2	8	7	1	5	4	6	3
6	5	4	9	3	2	7	1	8
7	3	1	4	6	8	2	5	9
8	1	2	3	5	6	9	7	4
5	7	6	8	4	9	1	3	2
3	4	9	1	2	7	6	8	5

36

4	8	6	1	7	9	2	5	3
7	3	5	4	6	2	9	8	1
9	2	1	3	8	5	4	7	6
3	1	9	6	5	4	8	2	7
2	6	8	9	1	7	5	3	4
5	7	4	8	2	3	6	1	9
8	4	7	5	9	1	3	6	2
6	9	2	7	3	8	1	4	5
1	5	3	2	4	6	7	9	8

Solutions

37

7	8	6	2	9	1	4	3	5
3	2	1	4	5	7	6	9	8
5	9	4	3	8	6	7	2	1
6	7	2	5	3	8	1	4	9
8	3	5	1	4	9	2	6	7
1	4	9	7	6	2	5	8	3
4	5	8	6	1	3	9	7	2
9	6	7	8	2	5	3	1	4
2	1	3	9	7	4	8	5	6

38

7	3	1	8	5	2	9	4	6
6	5	2	3	4	9	7	8	1
9	8	4	7	1	6	3	2	5
5	6	8	2	3	7	1	9	4
4	7	3	1	9	8	6	5	2
1	2	9	4	6	5	8	3	7
3	9	7	6	2	4	5	1	8
8	4	5	9	7	1	2	6	3
2	1	6	5	8	3	4	7	9

39

4	2	6	7	5	9	8	3	1
9	7	1	3	6	8	5	2	4
8	3	5	4	1	2	9	7	6
5	8	7	6	3	4	2	1	9
3	4	9	5	2	1	7	6	8
1	6	2	8	9	7	4	5	3
2	9	3	1	4	5	6	8	7
6	5	8	9	7	3	1	4	2
7	1	4	2	8	6	3	9	5

40

1	3	9	6	8	7	2	5	4
7	6	5	3	4	2	1	8	9
2	4	8	1	5	9	3	7	6
3	8	4	2	6	5	9	1	7
6	1	2	7	9	4	8	3	5
9	5	7	8	1	3	6	4	2
5	2	6	4	3	8	7	9	1
4	7	3	9	2	1	5	6	8
8	9	1	5	7	6	4	2	3

Solutions

41

6	1	7	9	2	3	5	4	8
2	8	5	1	7	4	6	3	9
3	4	9	8	6	5	2	7	1
7	5	6	3	1	8	4	9	2
4	2	8	6	5	9	7	1	3
1	9	3	2	4	7	8	6	5
9	6	2	4	8	1	3	5	7
8	7	1	5	3	6	9	2	4
5	3	4	7	9	2	1	8	6

42

4	6	1	9	3	7	5	2	8
9	5	3	2	1	8	4	7	6
7	2	8	4	5	6	1	3	9
1	4	5	7	9	2	8	6	3
6	9	7	3	8	4	2	5	1
3	8	2	1	6	5	7	9	4
5	3	6	8	7	1	9	4	2
2	1	9	5	4	3	6	8	7
8	7	4	6	2	9	3	1	5

43

9	2	3	8	4	7	5	6	1
1	7	6	5	9	2	3	8	4
8	4	5	6	1	3	7	2	9
2	9	8	4	6	5	1	7	3
4	3	7	2	8	1	9	5	6
5	6	1	3	7	9	2	4	8
6	5	2	9	3	8	4	1	7
3	1	4	7	2	6	8	9	5
7	8	9	1	5	4	6	3	2

44

6	3	4	8	7	2	5	1	9
9	8	1	4	6	5	7	3	2
7	5	2	9	3	1	8	6	4
1	4	8	3	9	7	6	2	5
2	7	6	5	8	4	3	9	1
3	9	5	2	1	6	4	8	7
4	6	7	1	2	3	9	5	8
8	2	3	7	5	9	1	4	6
5	1	9	6	4	8	2	7	3

Solutions

45

7	9	5	4	8	2	6	3	1
8	2	1	3	9	6	7	5	4
6	4	3	7	5	1	8	2	9
9	3	7	6	1	4	5	8	2
4	1	2	5	7	8	3	9	6
5	8	6	9	2	3	1	4	7
1	6	4	2	3	5	9	7	8
2	5	9	8	6	7	4	1	3
3	7	8	1	4	9	2	6	5

46

9	3	1	2	4	5	6	7	8
7	6	5	9	8	1	3	4	2
2	4	8	3	7	6	5	1	9
3	9	2	5	6	4	7	8	1
8	7	4	1	9	3	2	5	6
5	1	6	7	2	8	4	9	3
6	8	3	4	5	9	1	2	7
1	5	7	8	3	2	9	6	4
4	2	9	6	1	7	8	3	5

Solutions

47

6	8	9	7	1	2	3	5	4
3	1	5	6	4	8	7	2	9
4	7	2	5	3	9	1	6	8
9	4	3	1	2	7	6	8	5
1	6	8	9	5	3	2	4	7
5	2	7	8	6	4	9	3	1
8	5	6	2	7	1	4	9	3
7	9	4	3	8	6	5	1	2
2	3	1	4	9	5	8	7	6

48

3	5	6	2	7	9	1	8	4
2	9	8	6	4	1	7	5	3
1	4	7	5	8	3	6	9	2
7	2	9	1	5	4	3	6	8
8	3	4	9	6	2	5	1	7
6	1	5	7	3	8	2	4	9
5	7	2	8	9	6	4	3	1
4	8	1	3	2	5	9	7	6
9	6	3	4	1	7	8	2	5

Solutions

49

7	6	1	5	8	2	4	3	9
8	5	2	3	4	9	6	1	7
3	4	9	1	7	6	2	5	8
9	1	7	4	5	8	3	6	2
4	2	3	6	1	7	8	9	5
5	8	6	2	9	3	1	7	4
1	7	5	8	3	4	9	2	6
2	3	8	9	6	5	7	4	1
6	9	4	7	2	1	5	8	3

50

8	6	3	1	5	7	2	9	4
5	9	2	3	8	4	6	1	7
7	1	4	9	2	6	8	5	3
3	8	5	7	6	2	9	4	1
4	7	6	8	9	1	3	2	5
9	2	1	4	3	5	7	8	6
2	3	7	5	1	9	4	6	8
6	5	8	2	4	3	1	7	9
1	4	9	6	7	8	5	3	2

Solutions

51

4	7	6	3	5	8	9	1	2
1	8	2	9	4	7	3	6	5
3	5	9	2	1	6	8	7	4
5	9	4	7	3	1	6	2	8
2	6	3	5	8	9	1	4	7
7	1	8	4	6	2	5	3	9
8	4	7	6	9	3	2	5	1
9	3	5	1	2	4	7	8	6
6	2	1	8	7	5	4	9	3

52

3	9	5	4	6	8	1	2	7
7	4	1	2	9	3	5	8	6
6	2	8	1	5	7	4	3	9
9	5	6	3	1	4	8	7	2
2	7	4	5	8	6	3	9	1
8	1	3	9	7	2	6	5	4
4	8	9	6	2	5	7	1	3
5	6	2	7	3	1	9	4	8
1	3	7	8	4	9	2	6	5

Solutions

53

5	6	8	7	3	4	9	2	1
7	4	1	9	8	2	5	6	3
9	3	2	6	5	1	7	8	4
8	9	3	4	7	6	1	5	2
4	5	7	1	2	3	8	9	6
1	2	6	5	9	8	4	3	7
6	1	9	2	4	5	3	7	8
3	7	4	8	6	9	2	1	5
2	8	5	3	1	7	6	4	9

54

7	2	6	1	9	4	5	3	8
4	1	9	3	8	5	2	7	6
5	3	8	7	2	6	4	9	1
8	7	2	9	4	1	3	6	5
9	4	1	5	6	3	8	2	7
6	5	3	8	7	2	9	1	4
1	8	5	2	3	7	6	4	9
3	6	7	4	5	9	1	8	2
2	9	4	6	1	8	7	5	3

Solutions

55

9	2	7	6	4	1	5	3	8
1	6	4	5	3	8	7	9	2
8	3	5	2	7	9	6	1	4
4	7	1	8	5	2	9	6	3
5	8	2	3	9	6	4	7	1
6	9	3	4	1	7	2	8	5
2	4	9	1	6	3	8	5	7
3	5	6	7	8	4	1	2	9
7	1	8	9	2	5	3	4	6

56

2	1	3	9	8	5	4	7	6
5	4	8	6	1	7	9	2	3
9	7	6	2	3	4	8	1	5
4	6	7	3	2	8	1	5	9
8	5	1	7	6	9	3	4	2
3	2	9	4	5	1	7	6	8
6	9	2	1	7	3	5	8	4
1	8	4	5	9	2	6	3	7
7	3	5	8	4	6	2	9	1

Solutions

57

6	4	9	5	1	3	8	2	7
8	5	3	4	7	2	6	1	9
1	2	7	6	9	8	3	4	5
2	8	4	1	3	9	7	5	6
3	9	6	7	4	5	2	8	1
5	7	1	2	8	6	9	3	4
9	6	5	8	2	1	4	7	3
7	1	8	3	6	4	5	9	2
4	3	2	9	5	7	1	6	8

58

2	1	5	3	6	8	7	9	4
6	4	9	2	7	1	3	5	8
3	7	8	9	5	4	1	2	6
7	3	1	4	2	5	6	8	9
9	5	6	8	1	7	4	3	2
8	2	4	6	9	3	5	7	1
1	9	7	5	4	2	8	6	3
4	8	2	7	3	6	9	1	5
5	6	3	1	8	9	2	4	7

6	7	9	3	4	2	1	8	5
5	2	1	9	6	8	3	4	7
3	8	4	5	1	7	9	2	6
7	5	3	8	2	6	4	9	1
8	4	6	7	9	1	2	5	3
9	1	2	4	3	5	7	6	8
2	9	8	6	7	3	5	1	4
1	6	7	2	5	4	8	3	9
4	3	5	1	8	9	6	7	2

6	2	8	9	7	3	5	1	4
4	5	9	1	2	8	7	3	6
1	3	7	4	5	6	2	9	8
2	8	1	7	6	4	9	5	3
9	4	6	2	3	5	8	7	1
5	7	3	8	9	1	4	6	2
3	9	2	6	8	7	1	4	5
7	1	5	3	4	2	6	8	9
8	6	4	5	1	9	3	2	7

Solutions

61

8	1	4	9	2	6	7	3	5
9	6	3	5	8	7	2	1	4
7	5	2	4	3	1	9	8	6
4	3	7	1	5	9	8	6	2
1	8	6	2	7	3	5	4	9
2	9	5	6	4	8	1	7	3
3	7	9	8	6	5	4	2	1
6	4	1	7	9	2	3	5	8
5	2	8	3	1	4	6	9	7

62

1	4	3	9	8	6	7	2	5
2	9	8	1	7	5	3	4	6
7	6	5	4	2	3	1	8	9
5	8	6	2	9	1	4	7	3
4	3	7	5	6	8	2	9	1
9	1	2	3	4	7	6	5	8
8	7	9	6	1	2	5	3	4
3	2	1	8	5	4	9	6	7
6	5	4	7	3	9	8	1	2

Solutions

63

4	8	3	2	9	1	5	7	6
5	7	9	3	4	6	2	1	8
1	6	2	5	7	8	4	3	9
3	5	4	7	1	9	6	8	2
6	1	7	4	8	2	3	9	5
9	2	8	6	3	5	1	4	7
7	4	5	9	6	3	8	2	1
8	3	6	1	2	7	9	5	4
2	9	1	8	5	4	7	6	3

64

9	3	1	2	4	7	6	8	5
7	6	8	1	5	9	4	3	2
4	2	5	6	8	3	9	7	1
6	5	4	3	9	8	1	2	7
3	1	2	5	7	6	8	4	9
8	7	9	4	2	1	5	6	3
5	4	3	8	1	2	7	9	6
1	9	6	7	3	4	2	5	8
2	8	7	9	6	5	3	1	4

Solutions

65

7	1	2	4	9	3	5	8	6
5	4	3	6	1	8	7	2	9
8	9	6	2	5	7	1	4	3
3	5	1	8	4	2	6	9	7
4	6	7	5	3	9	8	1	2
2	8	9	7	6	1	3	5	4
6	2	5	1	7	4	9	3	8
9	7	4	3	8	5	2	6	1
1	3	8	9	2	6	4	7	5

66

2	5	3	9	7	4	1	8	6
1	7	9	6	8	2	4	3	5
6	4	8	5	3	1	7	9	2
7	1	2	8	6	9	3	5	4
8	9	6	4	5	3	2	1	7
4	3	5	1	2	7	8	6	9
5	2	7	3	1	6	9	4	8
9	8	1	7	4	5	6	2	3
3	6	4	2	9	8	5	7	1

2	9	7	8	3	6	5	1	4
5	6	1	4	2	9	8	7	3
4	8	3	1	5	7	2	6	9
1	4	2	7	8	5	9	3	6
7	5	8	9	6	3	1	4	2
9	3	6	2	1	4	7	5	8
3	2	4	5	7	8	6	9	1
6	1	5	3	9	2	4	8	7
8	7	9	6	4	1	3	2	5

7	9	2	1	5	4	8	3	6
5	3	4	9	8	6	7	1	2
8	1	6	7	2	3	9	4	5
4	7	3	8	1	2	6	5	9
1	8	5	6	4	9	3	2	7
6	2	9	5	3	7	1	8	4
3	6	8	4	7	5	2	9	1
9	5	1	2	6	8	4	7	3
2	4	7	3	9	1	5	6	8

Solutions

69

1	9	7	5	4	6	2	8	3
2	8	5	7	1	3	6	9	4
4	6	3	2	9	8	7	5	1
3	1	2	4	8	9	5	7	6
8	5	9	6	7	1	3	4	2
7	4	6	3	2	5	9	1	8
5	7	4	8	3	2	1	6	9
6	2	1	9	5	4	8	3	7
9	3	8	1	6	7	4	2	5

70

5	2	8	4	6	7	9	3	1
6	7	9	5	1	3	4	2	8
1	3	4	2	8	9	7	5	6
7	6	3	9	4	5	8	1	2
9	5	2	8	3	1	6	7	4
4	8	1	7	2	6	5	9	3
3	4	5	1	9	8	2	6	7
8	1	7	6	5	2	3	4	9
2	9	6	3	7	4	1	8	5

71

4	8	5	6	9	1	3	2	7
1	9	7	5	3	2	8	4	6
3	2	6	7	8	4	9	1	5
7	4	2	1	5	3	6	8	9
6	3	8	2	4	9	5	7	1
9	5	1	8	6	7	2	3	4
2	7	9	3	1	6	4	5	8
8	1	4	9	2	5	7	6	3
5	6	3	4	7	8	1	9	2

72

3	9	6	7	8	1	4	2	5
2	4	7	3	6	5	8	9	1
1	8	5	2	4	9	3	7	6
7	5	4	1	3	8	2	6	9
9	3	1	5	2	6	7	4	8
6	2	8	9	7	4	1	5	3
8	6	2	4	9	3	5	1	7
4	1	3	6	5	7	9	8	2
5	7	9	8	1	2	6	3	4

Solutions

73

7	5	8	3	6	1	9	4	2
4	6	3	7	9	2	8	1	5
9	1	2	5	4	8	6	3	7
3	4	1	6	5	9	2	7	8
5	8	7	2	3	4	1	6	9
6	2	9	1	8	7	3	5	4
1	9	4	8	7	3	5	2	6
8	3	6	4	2	5	7	9	1
2	7	5	9	1	6	4	8	3

74

2	7	1	5	3	4	8	9	6
3	9	8	1	2	6	7	4	5
6	4	5	9	8	7	1	3	2
9	2	6	3	4	8	5	1	7
7	5	4	6	9	1	2	8	3
8	1	3	7	5	2	9	6	4
1	8	2	4	6	5	3	7	9
4	3	7	2	1	9	6	5	8
5	6	9	8	7	3	4	2	1

Solutions

75

3	1	8	6	2	7	4	5	9
7	2	4	3	5	9	1	6	8
5	9	6	8	4	1	7	3	2
6	3	1	7	8	5	9	2	4
9	7	2	1	3	4	6	8	5
4	8	5	9	6	2	3	1	7
8	5	7	4	1	3	2	9	6
2	4	3	5	9	6	8	7	1
1	6	9	2	7	8	5	4	3

76

9	3	4	7	5	1	8	6	2
7	5	8	9	6	2	1	3	4
2	1	6	8	4	3	7	5	9
8	6	3	5	9	4	2	1	7
4	7	9	1	2	6	5	8	3
5	2	1	3	7	8	4	9	6
6	9	5	4	1	7	3	2	8
3	4	2	6	8	5	9	7	1
1	8	7	2	3	9	6	4	5

Solutions

77

4	5	7	8	2	9	3	1	6
2	6	3	4	7	1	8	9	5
1	9	8	3	5	6	4	2	7
9	3	6	5	1	8	2	7	4
8	7	4	9	3	2	5	6	1
5	1	2	7	6	4	9	3	8
6	8	5	2	9	7	1	4	3
7	4	9	1	8	3	6	5	2
3	2	1	6	4	5	7	8	9

78

1	5	9	2	4	3	7	6	8
3	4	8	1	6	7	2	9	5
7	6	2	9	8	5	4	1	3
4	9	6	8	5	2	3	7	1
5	3	1	6	7	4	8	2	9
2	8	7	3	1	9	5	4	6
8	2	5	4	9	1	6	3	7
6	1	4	7	3	8	9	5	2
9	7	3	5	2	6	1	8	4

Solutions

79

1	5	8	9	4	2	3	7	6
9	3	4	7	8	6	2	1	5
6	7	2	3	1	5	9	4	8
5	2	7	6	9	4	8	3	1
8	1	9	5	3	7	6	2	4
3	4	6	8	2	1	7	5	9
4	9	5	2	6	3	1	8	7
2	6	1	4	7	8	5	9	3
7	8	3	1	5	9	4	6	2

80

9	4	7	6	5	8	1	3	2
3	8	5	9	1	2	4	7	6
1	2	6	4	3	7	9	5	8
5	3	4	7	8	1	2	6	9
2	9	8	3	6	4	5	1	7
6	7	1	2	9	5	3	8	4
8	5	9	1	4	6	7	2	3
4	1	2	8	7	3	6	9	5
7	6	3	5	2	9	8	4	1

Solutions

81

9	6	1	8	7	2	3	4	5
2	3	5	4	1	6	9	8	7
4	7	8	9	5	3	2	1	6
6	9	3	1	8	7	4	5	2
8	1	2	6	4	5	7	9	3
5	4	7	3	2	9	1	6	8
1	8	6	2	3	4	5	7	9
3	5	4	7	9	8	6	2	1
7	2	9	5	6	1	8	3	4

82

8	6	5	7	4	1	3	2	9
4	2	1	9	3	6	8	5	7
7	9	3	5	2	8	4	6	1
9	4	6	1	5	2	7	8	3
2	3	7	8	6	4	9	1	5
1	5	8	3	7	9	6	4	2
3	8	2	4	1	7	5	9	6
6	7	4	2	9	5	1	3	8
5	1	9	6	8	3	2	7	4

83

2	9	5	6	1	8	4	7	3
4	6	1	3	5	7	8	9	2
7	8	3	4	9	2	6	1	5
5	7	4	8	6	1	2	3	9
1	2	8	7	3	9	5	4	6
9	3	6	2	4	5	1	8	7
6	4	9	5	8	3	7	2	1
8	1	2	9	7	6	3	5	4
3	5	7	1	2	4	9	6	8

84

4	6	7	9	2	8	3	5	1
2	5	3	6	1	7	8	9	4
9	8	1	3	5	4	2	6	7
5	9	2	4	3	6	1	7	8
8	1	4	5	7	2	9	3	6
7	3	6	1	8	9	5	4	2
6	7	8	2	9	5	4	1	3
3	2	5	7	4	1	6	8	9
1	4	9	8	6	3	7	2	5

Solutions

85

1	8	7	5	6	2	3	4	9
5	9	4	3	1	7	6	8	2
2	6	3	9	4	8	7	5	1
8	1	6	2	5	4	9	3	7
7	5	9	1	3	6	8	2	4
4	3	2	7	8	9	1	6	5
3	7	1	8	2	5	4	9	6
6	2	8	4	9	1	5	7	3
9	4	5	6	7	3	2	1	8

86

8	4	9	7	2	1	6	5	3
2	7	1	5	3	6	4	9	8
3	6	5	4	8	9	1	7	2
7	3	8	9	6	5	2	4	1
5	1	2	8	7	4	3	6	9
4	9	6	2	1	3	7	8	5
6	5	4	1	9	2	8	3	7
1	8	3	6	5	7	9	2	4
9	2	7	3	4	8	5	1	6

87

7	4	3	8	1	6	9	2	5
5	8	6	4	2	9	7	3	1
2	1	9	7	3	5	8	6	4
3	7	8	5	4	1	6	9	2
4	5	2	6	9	3	1	7	8
9	6	1	2	8	7	5	4	3
6	9	4	3	5	8	2	1	7
1	2	5	9	7	4	3	8	6
8	3	7	1	6	2	4	5	9

88

1	7	9	6	3	4	2	8	5
4	8	3	5	7	2	1	9	6
2	6	5	8	1	9	4	3	7
9	2	7	3	8	1	5	6	4
6	4	1	2	9	5	3	7	8
3	5	8	4	6	7	9	1	2
8	3	4	1	2	6	7	5	9
7	1	2	9	5	8	6	4	3
5	9	6	7	4	3	8	2	1

Solutions

89

8	4	3	7	6	9	1	2	5
5	2	6	3	8	1	9	4	7
1	9	7	2	5	4	3	8	6
6	1	9	5	3	8	4	7	2
2	3	4	1	7	6	5	9	8
7	8	5	9	4	2	6	3	1
4	6	2	8	9	5	7	1	3
3	5	8	4	1	7	2	6	9
9	7	1	6	2	3	8	5	4

90

9	5	6	2	8	3	4	1	7
8	2	7	5	4	1	3	6	9
4	3	1	9	7	6	2	5	8
2	8	9	6	3	7	1	4	5
6	1	4	8	5	2	9	7	3
5	7	3	1	9	4	8	2	6
7	6	2	3	1	8	5	9	4
3	4	5	7	2	9	6	8	1
1	9	8	4	6	5	7	3	2

Solutions

91

7	1	3	6	8	5	4	2	9
6	8	5	9	2	4	3	1	7
4	2	9	1	3	7	5	6	8
8	4	7	2	1	6	9	3	5
1	3	6	8	5	9	7	4	2
9	5	2	7	4	3	6	8	1
2	9	4	3	7	8	1	5	6
5	7	8	4	6	1	2	9	3
3	6	1	5	9	2	8	7	4

92

8	9	1	7	5	3	2	4	6
4	2	5	1	6	8	3	7	9
7	6	3	4	2	9	8	1	5
2	8	7	3	9	1	5	6	4
9	3	6	2	4	5	1	8	7
1	5	4	6	8	7	9	2	3
6	7	8	9	3	2	4	5	1
3	1	2	5	7	4	6	9	8
5	4	9	8	1	6	7	3	2

Solutions

93

9	2	5	1	6	3	7	4	8
7	3	1	8	9	4	2	5	6
8	4	6	2	7	5	3	9	1
5	7	9	3	1	2	6	8	4
1	8	4	7	5	6	9	2	3
2	6	3	9	4	8	1	7	5
6	5	7	4	3	9	8	1	2
4	9	8	6	2	1	5	3	7
3	1	2	5	8	7	4	6	9

94

9	4	7	2	5	1	6	3	8
8	1	3	6	4	9	7	2	5
2	5	6	3	8	7	9	1	4
4	2	8	5	9	6	3	7	1
3	6	5	7	1	2	8	4	9
1	7	9	4	3	8	2	5	6
5	3	2	9	6	4	1	8	7
6	8	4	1	7	3	5	9	2
7	9	1	8	2	5	4	6	3

95

7	5	1	6	2	8	3	4	9
2	6	3	5	4	9	7	1	8
8	9	4	3	7	1	6	2	5
3	2	5	4	8	7	1	9	6
9	1	8	2	5	6	4	7	3
4	7	6	9	1	3	8	5	2
5	8	2	1	6	4	9	3	7
1	3	7	8	9	2	5	6	4
6	4	9	7	3	5	2	8	1

96

5	1	7	8	6	2	3	4	9
9	8	2	1	3	4	6	5	7
4	6	3	5	7	9	1	2	8
3	5	8	2	1	6	7	9	4
2	7	1	9	4	3	8	6	5
6	9	4	7	8	5	2	3	1
7	4	5	6	2	8	9	1	3
8	3	6	4	9	1	5	7	2
1	2	9	3	5	7	4	8	6

Solutions

97

6	1	8	4	3	2	5	7	9
9	3	4	7	5	1	6	2	8
5	2	7	9	8	6	4	3	1
1	8	6	3	7	5	9	4	2
2	9	5	6	4	8	3	1	7
7	4	3	2	1	9	8	5	6
4	5	1	8	6	7	2	9	3
3	6	9	1	2	4	7	8	5
8	7	2	5	9	3	1	6	4

98

2	1	6	3	4	9	8	7	5
7	4	9	5	8	2	6	3	1
5	8	3	6	1	7	2	4	9
6	9	4	2	3	8	1	5	7
3	2	8	1	7	5	4	9	6
1	7	5	9	6	4	3	8	2
8	6	2	7	9	3	5	1	4
4	5	7	8	2	1	9	6	3
9	3	1	4	5	6	7	2	8

Solutions

99

2	9	8	3	7	5	6	4	1
5	6	7	8	1	4	2	3	9
3	1	4	6	9	2	8	5	7
4	3	6	1	8	7	5	9	2
9	7	2	5	6	3	4	1	8
8	5	1	4	2	9	7	6	3
6	8	9	7	5	1	3	2	4
1	4	5	2	3	8	9	7	6
7	2	3	9	4	6	1	8	5

100

1	6	7	9	8	4	2	5	3
8	4	5	2	3	6	7	1	9
2	9	3	7	5	1	4	6	8
3	5	1	4	2	8	6	9	7
9	8	4	5	6	7	1	3	2
7	2	6	3	1	9	5	8	4
5	1	9	8	4	2	3	7	6
6	7	2	1	9	3	8	4	5
4	3	8	6	7	5	9	2	1

Solutions

101

1	2	8	4	7	6	5	9	3
4	5	6	2	9	3	8	1	7
3	7	9	1	5	8	2	6	4
2	9	4	5	3	7	1	8	6
5	3	1	8	6	2	7	4	9
8	6	7	9	1	4	3	5	2
7	1	3	6	4	5	9	2	8
9	4	2	7	8	1	6	3	5
6	8	5	3	2	9	4	7	1

102

8	6	3	4	7	1	9	5	2
7	4	1	5	9	2	8	6	3
2	5	9	8	6	3	4	7	1
1	3	8	2	5	7	6	4	9
6	9	5	1	8	4	2	3	7
4	2	7	9	3	6	5	1	8
3	8	4	6	1	9	7	2	5
5	7	2	3	4	8	1	9	6
9	1	6	7	2	5	3	8	4

103

4	9	2	5	8	1	6	3	7
1	5	8	3	7	6	9	4	2
7	6	3	4	2	9	1	8	5
2	8	9	6	5	3	7	1	4
6	7	4	1	9	2	8	5	3
5	3	1	8	4	7	2	6	9
9	1	6	7	3	5	4	2	8
3	4	7	2	6	8	5	9	1
8	2	5	9	1	4	3	7	6

104

5	3	2	8	4	7	9	6	1
6	4	7	2	9	1	5	3	8
9	8	1	5	3	6	2	4	7
2	7	3	9	6	5	8	1	4
8	1	9	7	2	4	6	5	3
4	5	6	3	1	8	7	2	9
3	2	5	1	7	9	4	8	6
7	6	8	4	5	3	1	9	2
1	9	4	6	8	2	3	7	5

Solutions

105

3	7	9	4	2	1	5	6	8
2	8	4	6	9	5	3	7	1
1	6	5	3	7	8	9	4	2
5	2	8	1	3	7	6	9	4
7	9	3	2	4	6	1	8	5
4	1	6	5	8	9	7	2	3
9	5	2	7	1	4	8	3	6
6	3	7	8	5	2	4	1	9
8	4	1	9	6	3	2	5	7

106

3	2	7	9	8	6	1	4	5
5	9	8	7	4	1	2	3	6
1	4	6	3	2	5	7	9	8
8	3	9	1	5	7	6	2	4
6	7	1	2	9	4	5	8	3
4	5	2	6	3	8	9	7	1
2	6	3	4	1	9	8	5	7
7	8	4	5	6	2	3	1	9
9	1	5	8	7	3	4	6	2

107

9	2	8	6	5	3	4	1	7
1	4	6	2	8	7	9	5	3
3	7	5	4	9	1	2	8	6
4	3	2	5	6	8	7	9	1
8	5	7	9	1	4	3	6	2
6	1	9	3	7	2	8	4	5
7	8	3	1	4	6	5	2	9
2	9	1	8	3	5	6	7	4
5	6	4	7	2	9	1	3	8

108

1	9	4	6	2	3	8	7	5
7	6	5	9	1	8	3	4	2
8	2	3	4	5	7	9	6	1
9	5	7	1	3	2	4	8	6
3	8	6	5	4	9	2	1	7
2	4	1	7	8	6	5	9	3
4	7	9	3	6	5	1	2	8
5	1	2	8	7	4	6	3	9
6	3	8	2	9	1	7	5	4

Solutions

2	6	4	1	5	8	3	7	9
9	7	8	4	3	2	5	1	6
1	3	5	9	6	7	4	2	8
3	5	9	2	7	6	8	4	1
8	1	2	3	4	5	9	6	7
7	4	6	8	1	9	2	5	3
4	8	3	6	2	1	7	9	5
6	9	7	5	8	4	1	3	2
5	2	1	7	9	3	6	8	4

7	2	1	3	8	4	5	6	9
9	4	5	7	6	2	1	3	8
8	3	6	5	1	9	4	2	7
6	7	9	2	4	5	8	1	3
5	1	2	8	3	6	9	7	4
3	8	4	1	9	7	2	5	6
4	6	7	9	2	1	3	8	5
2	9	8	6	5	3	7	4	1
1	5	3	4	7	8	6	9	2

111

6	8	2	5	4	9	7	3	1
9	7	4	2	1	3	8	5	6
3	1	5	7	6	8	4	2	9
8	2	6	1	3	7	9	4	5
1	9	3	4	2	5	6	7	8
5	4	7	9	8	6	3	1	2
2	6	8	3	5	4	1	9	7
4	5	9	8	7	1	2	6	3
7	3	1	6	9	2	5	8	4

112

2	9	6	8	3	1	7	5	4
7	3	5	9	4	6	1	8	2
4	8	1	2	5	7	6	3	9
6	7	4	3	9	8	2	1	5
8	1	2	6	7	5	9	4	3
9	5	3	4	1	2	8	7	6
5	2	9	1	8	4	3	6	7
3	4	8	7	6	9	5	2	1
1	6	7	5	2	3	4	9	8

Solutions

113

9	2	4	6	7	5	1	8	3
7	6	8	4	1	3	9	2	5
3	1	5	8	9	2	7	6	4
4	9	1	3	8	6	5	7	2
5	8	7	2	4	1	6	3	9
6	3	2	9	5	7	4	1	8
1	5	9	7	2	8	3	4	6
2	4	6	1	3	9	8	5	7
8	7	3	5	6	4	2	9	1

114

7	9	1	5	6	8	2	3	4
5	3	6	7	4	2	9	1	8
4	2	8	1	3	9	6	7	5
1	6	4	2	5	7	3	8	9
8	7	9	6	1	3	5	4	2
2	5	3	9	8	4	7	6	1
6	1	2	4	7	5	8	9	3
9	8	7	3	2	1	4	5	6
3	4	5	8	9	6	1	2	7

Solutions

115

8	2	3	4	5	6	9	7	1
1	7	9	3	2	8	5	4	6
6	4	5	7	9	1	3	8	2
9	8	2	1	6	3	4	5	7
5	1	6	9	7	4	8	2	3
7	3	4	5	8	2	1	6	9
3	9	8	6	4	7	2	1	5
4	6	1	2	3	5	7	9	8
2	5	7	8	1	9	6	3	4

116

2	3	8	6	9	4	1	7	5
9	5	1	7	2	8	4	6	3
4	7	6	1	5	3	2	9	8
3	2	7	8	4	1	9	5	6
1	9	4	5	7	6	3	8	2
8	6	5	2	3	9	7	1	4
5	8	3	4	1	7	6	2	9
7	4	2	9	6	5	8	3	1
6	1	9	3	8	2	5	4	7

Solutions

117

9	6	7	1	2	5	3	4	8
4	2	1	9	8	3	5	6	7
5	8	3	7	6	4	9	1	2
3	9	5	4	1	8	7	2	6
1	4	6	3	7	2	8	5	9
8	7	2	6	5	9	4	3	1
6	3	4	2	9	7	1	8	5
2	5	9	8	4	1	6	7	3
7	1	8	5	3	6	2	9	4

118

1	4	5	3	6	9	7	8	2
8	3	2	7	5	1	4	6	9
7	9	6	4	2	8	5	1	3
6	2	4	1	8	3	9	7	5
5	1	3	9	7	2	8	4	6
9	8	7	5	4	6	2	3	1
3	6	8	2	9	4	1	5	7
4	5	9	6	1	7	3	2	8
2	7	1	8	3	5	6	9	4

Solutions

119

8	6	5	3	2	1	7	4	9
2	9	4	7	8	5	6	3	1
1	7	3	9	4	6	8	2	5
4	3	1	5	6	2	9	7	8
7	8	2	1	9	4	3	5	6
9	5	6	8	7	3	2	1	4
3	4	7	6	1	8	5	9	2
5	1	8	2	3	9	4	6	7
6	2	9	4	5	7	1	8	3

120

3	8	5	9	2	4	1	6	7
4	6	7	5	3	1	2	9	8
1	2	9	7	6	8	5	3	4
9	1	4	2	5	7	6	8	3
8	3	2	6	1	9	4	7	5
7	5	6	8	4	3	9	2	1
2	7	3	1	9	5	8	4	6
6	4	1	3	8	2	7	5	9
5	9	8	4	7	6	3	1	2

Solutions

121

2	7	8	3	9	1	5	6	4
3	6	4	2	5	7	8	1	9
1	5	9	8	4	6	7	3	2
9	1	7	5	6	3	4	2	8
4	8	5	7	1	2	6	9	3
6	3	2	9	8	4	1	5	7
5	2	1	4	7	9	3	8	6
8	4	3	6	2	5	9	7	1
7	9	6	1	3	8	2	4	5

122

4	5	8	3	7	9	6	2	1
6	9	3	2	1	5	7	8	4
2	7	1	4	6	8	9	5	3
8	3	4	6	9	7	2	1	5
1	2	7	5	3	4	8	9	6
9	6	5	8	2	1	3	4	7
7	1	6	9	5	2	4	3	8
5	4	9	7	8	3	1	6	2
3	8	2	1	4	6	5	7	9

123

7	2	4	5	3	1	8	9	6
1	3	5	6	8	9	7	4	2
9	8	6	2	7	4	3	5	1
8	4	1	9	6	2	5	3	7
3	6	2	7	5	8	4	1	9
5	9	7	4	1	3	6	2	8
4	7	9	3	2	6	1	8	5
6	1	3	8	9	5	2	7	4
2	5	8	1	4	7	9	6	3

124

3	8	1	5	9	2	7	4	6
7	6	2	8	1	4	9	5	3
5	9	4	3	6	7	2	8	1
6	2	8	9	3	5	1	7	4
9	7	3	6	4	1	8	2	5
1	4	5	2	7	8	3	6	9
2	5	6	1	8	3	4	9	7
8	3	7	4	5	9	6	1	2
4	1	9	7	2	6	5	3	8

Solutions

125

2	9	7	4	8	1	3	5	6
3	1	4	2	6	5	9	7	8
5	8	6	9	7	3	2	4	1
6	7	5	1	9	8	4	3	2
9	4	8	5	3	2	6	1	7
1	2	3	6	4	7	5	8	9
8	3	2	7	5	9	1	6	4
7	6	1	3	2	4	8	9	5
4	5	9	8	1	6	7	2	3

126

5	2	6	1	8	4	7	3	9
8	1	7	9	6	3	4	2	5
3	9	4	5	2	7	1	8	6
6	7	8	4	9	1	3	5	2
9	3	1	7	5	2	6	4	8
2	4	5	8	3	6	9	7	1
7	6	2	3	1	8	5	9	4
1	5	3	2	4	9	8	6	7
4	8	9	6	7	5	2	1	3

Solutions

127

8	3	4	6	5	9	7	1	2
6	5	7	4	2	1	8	3	9
1	2	9	7	8	3	6	5	4
5	9	6	3	4	7	2	8	1
4	1	8	9	6	2	5	7	3
2	7	3	8	1	5	4	9	6
9	4	5	2	3	8	1	6	7
7	6	1	5	9	4	3	2	8
3	8	2	1	7	6	9	4	5

128

6	3	8	2	5	4	9	7	1
5	1	7	3	8	9	6	2	4
9	4	2	1	7	6	5	3	8
8	7	1	6	4	3	2	9	5
3	2	5	7	9	8	1	4	6
4	6	9	5	1	2	7	8	3
2	5	3	4	6	7	8	1	9
1	8	4	9	2	5	3	6	7
7	9	6	8	3	1	4	5	2

Solutions

129

5	4	3	1	9	8	6	7	2
2	7	9	4	5	6	8	3	1
1	6	8	7	2	3	9	4	5
7	1	2	9	8	5	4	6	3
6	9	5	2	3	4	1	8	7
8	3	4	6	7	1	5	2	9
4	8	7	5	1	2	3	9	6
3	2	1	8	6	9	7	5	4
9	5	6	3	4	7	2	1	8

130

3	5	2	8	6	4	1	7	9
7	8	6	5	9	1	2	4	3
9	4	1	3	2	7	5	6	8
5	2	3	4	7	8	9	1	6
1	6	9	2	3	5	4	8	7
8	7	4	6	1	9	3	5	2
2	1	5	9	8	6	7	3	4
6	3	7	1	4	2	8	9	5
4	9	8	7	5	3	6	2	1

Solutions

131

9	3	2	1	4	6	8	5	7
7	1	8	9	5	3	6	4	2
5	6	4	8	7	2	1	9	3
2	7	3	5	1	4	9	6	8
6	4	9	3	8	7	5	2	1
8	5	1	2	6	9	7	3	4
1	9	6	4	3	8	2	7	5
4	2	5	7	9	1	3	8	6
3	8	7	6	2	5	4	1	9

132

6	1	8	3	9	2	4	7	5
4	2	5	8	1	7	9	3	6
7	9	3	4	5	6	1	2	8
5	6	4	1	8	3	7	9	2
9	7	1	5	2	4	8	6	3
8	3	2	6	7	9	5	4	1
3	5	9	7	6	1	2	8	4
2	8	6	9	4	5	3	1	7
1	4	7	2	3	8	6	5	9

Solutions

133

4	5	2	6	7	9	1	8	3
6	9	1	2	3	8	4	7	5
7	3	8	4	1	5	6	2	9
9	8	5	3	4	2	7	1	6
3	7	4	8	6	1	5	9	2
1	2	6	5	9	7	8	3	4
8	1	3	9	5	6	2	4	7
2	6	9	7	8	4	3	5	1
5	4	7	1	2	3	9	6	8

134

4	7	3	1	9	8	2	5	6
8	2	9	6	7	5	1	3	4
1	5	6	4	2	3	9	7	8
9	3	4	2	5	7	8	6	1
2	6	1	3	8	4	7	9	5
7	8	5	9	6	1	3	4	2
3	1	7	8	4	6	5	2	9
6	9	8	5	3	2	4	1	7
5	4	2	7	1	9	6	8	3

Solutions

135

4	5	2	7	6	9	3	1	8
7	6	8	5	3	1	2	9	4
1	3	9	2	8	4	6	5	7
9	1	5	4	7	6	8	2	3
8	2	6	1	9	3	4	7	5
3	4	7	8	2	5	1	6	9
2	9	4	3	1	7	5	8	6
6	8	3	9	5	2	7	4	1
5	7	1	6	4	8	9	3	2

136

3	2	5	6	4	8	7	1	9
6	7	8	2	9	1	5	4	3
9	4	1	5	3	7	2	6	8
8	3	9	7	1	2	6	5	4
2	6	7	4	8	5	3	9	1
1	5	4	3	6	9	8	2	7
5	9	2	1	7	3	4	8	6
4	8	3	9	5	6	1	7	2
7	1	6	8	2	4	9	3	5

Solutions

137

5	3	2	4	6	9	7	8	1
7	1	4	5	3	8	2	6	9
6	9	8	1	7	2	3	4	5
8	7	9	3	4	5	1	2	6
4	5	3	6	2	1	8	9	7
2	6	1	8	9	7	4	5	3
1	4	6	2	5	3	9	7	8
3	2	7	9	8	6	5	1	4
9	8	5	7	1	4	6	3	2

138

3	4	9	8	2	7	6	1	5
6	5	1	9	3	4	7	2	8
8	7	2	6	5	1	4	3	9
2	6	4	3	7	8	5	9	1
5	1	7	2	6	9	3	8	4
9	8	3	1	4	5	2	6	7
4	3	8	5	9	6	1	7	2
1	2	5	7	8	3	9	4	6
7	9	6	4	1	2	8	5	3

Solutions

139

3	1	8	9	6	5	2	4	7
7	4	2	3	8	1	5	9	6
6	9	5	7	4	2	8	1	3
8	6	3	2	9	7	4	5	1
1	5	9	4	3	6	7	8	2
2	7	4	5	1	8	6	3	9
9	2	6	1	5	4	3	7	8
4	3	7	8	2	9	1	6	5
5	8	1	6	7	3	9	2	4

140

2	8	5	1	7	6	3	4	9
9	1	7	8	4	3	2	5	6
3	4	6	9	2	5	8	7	1
5	7	8	3	1	4	6	9	2
6	9	2	5	8	7	1	3	4
4	3	1	2	6	9	5	8	7
1	6	3	4	9	8	7	2	5
7	5	9	6	3	2	4	1	8
8	2	4	7	5	1	9	6	3

Solutions

141

7	3	2	6	5	9	4	1	8
5	9	6	8	1	4	3	7	2
4	1	8	2	7	3	6	9	5
6	4	1	7	2	5	9	8	3
9	5	3	4	8	6	7	2	1
8	2	7	3	9	1	5	6	4
2	6	9	5	3	8	1	4	7
3	8	4	1	6	7	2	5	9
1	7	5	9	4	2	8	3	6

142

8	3	2	5	6	4	9	1	7
6	1	5	9	8	7	3	2	4
4	9	7	1	2	3	5	6	8
1	5	3	6	9	8	7	4	2
2	7	6	3	4	5	1	8	9
9	4	8	7	1	2	6	3	5
7	6	4	2	5	1	8	9	3
5	8	9	4	3	6	2	7	1
3	2	1	8	7	9	4	5	6

143

8	3	4	2	1	7	5	6	9
7	9	5	4	6	3	8	2	1
2	6	1	8	9	5	3	4	7
4	5	7	3	2	6	9	1	8
9	8	2	7	5	1	6	3	4
3	1	6	9	4	8	2	7	5
5	7	3	6	8	4	1	9	2
6	2	8	1	7	9	4	5	3
1	4	9	5	3	2	7	8	6

144

4	5	8	7	6	1	3	2	9
7	9	2	8	3	5	6	4	1
1	3	6	4	2	9	7	5	8
6	8	1	5	9	7	2	3	4
9	7	4	3	8	2	1	6	5
3	2	5	6	1	4	8	9	7
2	4	7	1	5	3	9	8	6
8	1	3	9	4	6	5	7	2
5	6	9	2	7	8	4	1	3

Solutions

145

6	4	9	3	8	1	7	5	2
3	1	8	7	5	2	6	4	9
5	2	7	6	4	9	8	1	3
4	7	3	9	2	6	5	8	1
2	8	5	1	7	4	3	9	6
9	6	1	8	3	5	4	2	7
1	9	4	5	6	7	2	3	8
8	5	6	2	1	3	9	7	4
7	3	2	4	9	8	1	6	5

146

7	8	2	3	9	4	5	1	6
4	9	1	5	6	8	7	3	2
6	5	3	2	7	1	9	8	4
1	4	8	7	5	3	6	2	9
2	6	5	8	1	9	3	4	7
9	3	7	4	2	6	1	5	8
8	7	4	6	3	5	2	9	1
5	2	9	1	8	7	4	6	3
3	1	6	9	4	2	8	7	5

Solutions

147

8	2	6	7	4	1	3	9	5
1	7	9	6	3	5	2	8	4
5	3	4	2	9	8	7	1	6
2	4	1	5	7	9	8	6	3
9	6	3	4	8	2	5	7	1
7	8	5	3	1	6	4	2	9
3	9	2	8	6	4	1	5	7
6	5	7	1	2	3	9	4	8
4	1	8	9	5	7	6	3	2

148

4	9	6	2	1	8	3	7	5
5	1	3	6	9	7	4	8	2
2	7	8	3	5	4	9	6	1
7	3	5	4	2	9	6	1	8
6	4	1	5	8	3	7	2	9
8	2	9	7	6	1	5	3	4
9	5	7	1	3	2	8	4	6
1	8	4	9	7	6	2	5	3
3	6	2	8	4	5	1	9	7

Solutions

149

9	4	1	7	6	3	5	8	2
8	3	2	1	4	5	9	7	6
7	5	6	8	2	9	3	4	1
5	1	7	3	9	2	8	6	4
3	2	4	6	7	8	1	9	5
6	8	9	4	5	1	7	2	3
1	6	8	9	3	4	2	5	7
4	9	5	2	1	7	6	3	8
2	7	3	5	8	6	4	1	9

150

8	6	3	5	4	2	1	9	7
7	2	4	1	9	6	8	3	5
5	1	9	7	8	3	2	4	6
2	5	6	8	3	9	7	1	4
4	3	8	6	1	7	5	2	9
9	7	1	2	5	4	6	8	3
6	4	2	9	7	1	3	5	8
3	8	7	4	2	5	9	6	1
1	9	5	3	6	8	4	7	2

Solutions

HOW MUCH SU DOKU CAN YOU DO?

978-0-06-137317-6

978-0-06-137318-3

978-0-06-137319-0

AND LOOK FOR OUR NEW SU DOKU SERIES

**NEW YORK POST
BATHROOM SU DOKU**
978-0-06-123973-1

**NEW YORK POST
CUBICLE SU DOKU**
978-0-06-123972-4

**NEW YORK POST
LOVE CAN WAIT
SU DOKU**
978-0-06-123971-7

**NEW YORK POST
PLANES, TRAINS,
AND SU DOKU**
978-0-06-123268-8

**NEW YORK POST
THE DOCTOR WILL
SEE YOU IN A MINUTE
SU DOKU**
978-0-06-123970-0

**NEW YORK POST
FAT-FREE SU DOKU**
978-0-06-123974-8

Puzzles by Pappocom presents

www.sudoku.com

the Su Doku website for all Su Doku fans. Check
it out for tips on solving, and for all the latest
news in the world of Sudoku.

Want more puzzles
of your favorite grade?

For an endless supply of the best Su Doku
puzzles get the **Sudoku program** for your
Windows PC. Download a 28-day free
try-out version of the program from
www.sudoku.com/download.htm

*Here's what you can do with the computer program
that you cannot do with pencil and paper:*

- Never run out of the grade of puzzle you
  enjoy the most
- Check whether your answer is correct with just
  one click
- Elect to be alerted if you make a wrong entry
- Delete numbers easily, with just a click
- Elect to have your puzzles timed, automatically
- Get hints, if you need them
- Replay the same puzzle, as many times as
  you like